CITIES OF THE
WORLD

AMSTERDAM

BY DEBORAH KENT

CHILDREN'S PRESS®
A Division of Grolier Publishing
New York London Hong Kong Sydney
Danbury, Connecticut

CONSULTANTS

Anneke Prins, Ph.D.
Native of Amsterdam
Professor of Dutch Language
Columbia University, New York City

Linda Cornwell
Learning Resource Consultant
Indiana Department of Education

Project Editor: Downing Publishing Services
Design Director: Karen Kohn & Associates, Ltd.
Photo Researcher: Jan Izzo
Pronunciations: Courtesy of Tony Breed, M.A., Linguistics, University of Chicago,
with help from Lamberdina Smith, Dutch Language Instructor

NOTES ON DUTCH PRONUNCIATION

The Dutch words in this book are pronounced basically the way the pronunciation
guides look. There are a few notes, however: *ah* is like *a* in father; *a* is as in can; *ay*
is as in day; *aw* is as in draw; *mare* sounds like mayor—it doesn't rhyme with air;
ow is always as in cow, never as in tow. There are some sounds in Dutch that do not
occur in English. Notice how you hold your lips to say "oo," and then notice where
you put your tongue to say "ay"; to pronounce *ooh*, say "oo" as in book, but move your
tongue forward to say "ay." *H* is like *h* as in hat, but stronger and harsher. If you try to
say *k* as in kite, but relax and slur the sound, it will sound like *h*. Ss-*h* should not sound
like *sh* as in ship; it is two sounds in a row: *ss* as in kiss, followed by *h*.

Library of Congress Cataloging-in-Publication Data
Kent, Deborah.
      Amsterdam / by Deborah Kent.
        p. cm. — (Cities of the world)
      Includes index.
      Summary: Describes the history, culture, daily life, and points of interest of
the capital and largest city in the Netherlands, a city that rests almost entirely
on wooden posts and is crisscrossed by dozens of canals.
     ISBN 0-516-20299-5 (lib. bdg.)   0-516-26141-x (pbk.)
     1. Amsterdam (Netherlands)—Juvenile literature. [1. Amsterdam
(Netherlands)] I. Title. II. Series: Cities of the world (New York, N.Y.)
DJ411.A53K46 1997   96-31988
949.2'352—dc20   CIP
                                                  AC

TABLE OF CONTENTS

S Q U A R E

On a bright summer morning, Amsterdam's Dam Square throngs with people. Parents push babies in strollers. Older children play tag or toss a ball back and forth. Dogs are everywhere, frisking along on their leashes.

Above the square looms the Royal Palace, one of the most ornate buildings in the city. Its outer walls are decorated with carvings of sea monsters and warriors. Inside, the pillared halls are adorned with paintings and statues. This artwork dates back 300 years. The Royal Family of the Netherlands does not actually live in the palace. Queen Beatrix, the nation's reigning monarch, does come here for special ceremonies every year.

When the Royal Palace was completed in 1655, Amsterdam was the richest city on earth. It was the heart of the region known as the Low Countries, consisting of present-day Belgium and the Netherlands. The Low Countries had colonies all over the world. Ships sailed into Amsterdam Harbor heavy with precious cargo. They brought spices from the South Seas, gold from South Africa, and furs and timber from North American forests.

Originally, the Royal Palace served as the seat of Amsterdam's city government. It was the biggest, most splendid city hall in all of Europe. It boasted to the world, "I am the wealthiest, the bravest, the strongest of cities!"

The Royal Palace

The Magic Number

Built upon marshy soil, the Royal Palace is supported by an enormous raft of wooden piles. These piles, the trunks of strong, tall trees, were driven deep into the ground beneath the foundation. Nearly every child in Amsterdam knows that 13,659 piles hold up the palace. The number is easy to remember. Take the number of days in the year—365. Add a *1* at the beginning and a 9 at the end. There it is, Amsterdam's magic number.

Today, the Netherlands is no longer a mighty world power. Amsterdam has ceased to be a fabulous Golden Age port. Yet it remains a city rich in art and history. Its people come from every continent, carrying their diverse cultures and traditions. Amsterdam is one of the most tolerant cities on earth. Here, every lifestyle and belief finds acceptance.

Atop the central cupola of the Royal Palace, a giant weathervane turns in the wind. It is shaped like a ship in full sail. The ship represents Amsterdam's magnificent past as a port of trade. But it is also a symbol of the city today, home to people who have traveled from so many distant nations. As it changes with the times, Amsterdam continues to grow and prosper. The weathervane seems to promise a future with favorable winds.

Feeding the pigeons at Dam Square

On top of the central cupola of the Royal Palace, this weathervane turns in the wind.

Almost as soon as they learn to walk, most children in Amsterdam are taught to swim. Their parents want to make sure they will know what to do if they should fall into the water unexpectedly. In Amsterdam, the water is never far away. Water has shaped the city, and the people of Amsterdam give it their love and respect.

"A CITY COMMON TO ALL"

Amsterdam has sometimes been called "the Venice of the North." Like Venice, Italy, Amsterdam is threaded with canals. Amsterdam's canals act as streets and avenues. Some are as broad as a four-lane highway. Others are as narrow as a one-way side street.

The city of Amsterdam is built upon some 90 islands, linked by about 600 bridges. Most of the islands were created by human beings. To the west of the city lies the North Sea. The IJ, a branch of the lake called the IJsselmeer, flanks the city's east side. Before the IJsselmeer was closed off by a dike, it was known as the Zuider Zee. In the past, boats

This view of Amsterdam shows the Herengracht (the Heren Canal).
The other two main canals in the city are the Keizersgracht and the Prinsengracht.

slipped through the canals, carrying goods to and from the harbor. Today, glass-topped canal boats churn their way through the city, loaded with camera-wielding tourists.

During the 1960s, the Netherlands did not have enough workers to run its factories and other industries. The nation welcomed thousands of foreign "guest workers." These "guests" were willing to work for relatively low wages. Many of them came from Turkey and Morocco. Other immigrants flocked to Amsterdam from former Dutch colonies. They poured in from Indonesia, from the Antilles in the West Indies, and from Suriname in South America. Some of these newcomers stayed for only a few years. They saved money and returned to their native lands. Most, however, made Amsterdam their permanent home.

IJ (AY)
IJsselmeer (AY-SELL-MARE)
Zuider Zee (ZOW-DER ZAY)
Herengracht (HEER-EH-HRAHHT)
Keizersgracht (KAY-ZERSS-HRAHHT)
Prinsengracht (PRINN-SUH-HRAHHT)

Tourists in glass-topped canal boats (right) use cameras like the one shown above to take pictures of Amsterdam's gabled houses.

Today, about 25 percent of all Amsterdammers are of non-European heritage. Like immigrants the world over, these newcomers try to hold onto their languages and traditions. But they quickly adopt Dutch customs as well. In the end, they are not Turks or Surinamese, but citizens of Amsterdam.

In Amsterdam, this blending of peoples is nothing new. Ever since the 1600s, Amsterdam has attracted people from many nations. One seventeenth-century visitor wrote, "It appears at first not to be a city of any particular people, but to be common to all."

In terms of population, Amsterdam is a medium-sized city. With some 700,000 people, it is about the same size as Boston or San Francisco. Amsterdam is also small in area. Its people live at very close quarters. Perhaps this is why they have learned to get along with one another. For the most part, they are not dismayed by differences in language, customs, and values. Amsterdammers sum up the spirit of their city with the Dutch word *gezellig*. *Gezellig* means "cozy and intimate." Nothing can be more gezellig than sipping coffee in a cafe in one of Amsterdam's old neighborhoods.

About 25 percent of Amsterdammers are of non-European heritage.

Shopping along the Damrak, a street that leads from Dam Square

Dining Out

The people of Amsterdam love dogs and cats. Pets are welcome nearly everywhere, even in the city's restaurants and shops. Amsterdam's dogs and cats rarely get into spats. Like the people, they are remarkably tolerant.

gezelllig (HUH-ZELL-IHH)
Damrak (DUMM-RAHK)

THE OLD AND THE NEW

Every evening after work, the men and women of Amsterdam gather in "brown cafes." They sit with friends and neighbors, eating, joking, and sharing the news of the day. Instead of tablecloths, thick rugs cover the tables. The ceiling is stained a warm, deep brown from years of tobacco smoke and dust. It is this typical brown color that gives the cafes their nickname. In the older sections of Amsterdam, a brown cafe stands on nearly every block.

At the height of Amsterdam's power during the seventeenth century, wealthy merchants built their homes along the city's main canals. The wider the

This man is selling eels, a favorite Amsterdam snack, to customers in one of the city's "brown cafes."

house was, the more taxes its owner had to pay. To avoid taxes, the merchants built their houses tall, deep, and very narrow. These houses lined the canals, standing side by side like the teeth of a comb. The steeply peaked roofs were adorned with gables and carvings. These handsome houses are still among the most prestigious addresses in Amsterdam.

Details of some Amsterdam roofs

Boats on the Waalseiland-gracht, an Amsterdam canal

One of Amsterdam's most interesting sections is the Jordaan. In the past, the Jordaan was among Amsterdam's poorest neighborhoods. Many of the people in the Jordaan worked as street peddlers. They sold fish, strawberries, or ribbons, pushing rickety carts and shouting their wares from door to door. Others held the lowliest job in the city—they cleaned the privies, or outdoor toilets. With its narrow streets, the Jordaan seems quaint and picturesque today. Boutiques and ethnic restaurants sprang up during the 1980s and 1990s. Many poor families still live in the Jordaan, but it also attracts artists, writers, and young professionals.

The Pijp is a noisy, crowded neighborhood of immigrant families. The streets are so narrow that they resemble tunnels. Poverty stalks the Pijp, as newcomers struggle for a toehold in a strange land. But in springtime, even the poorest home is brightened by windowboxes full of flowers.

In the spring and summer, nearly every home in the Pijp has a windowbox full of spring flowers.

Strawberries

Jordaan (YORE-DAN)
Pijp (PAYP)

In the southern and western sections of Amsterdam stand vast blocks of modern apartment buildings. They were constructed during a desperate housing shortage after World War II. Some were built around gardens and playgrounds. They create comfortable spaces where families can gather and have fun. Yet residents are still heard to complain that something is missing. These carefully planned communities lack the warmth of the old neighborhoods with their brown cafes.

Above: Residents of Amsterdam's new planned communities miss the warmth of these comfortable cafes in the older neighborhoods.

Moving Day

High above the door of every canal house extends a steel beam. At the tip of the beam is a hook, to which a pulley can be attached. This pulley system is vital to Amsterdam moving crews. Canal houses have steep, narrow stairways. It is almost impossible to move furniture from one floor to another. Furniture must be hoisted up on the beam. The movers then swing it in through wide windows designed precisely for this purpose.

LIVING DAY TO DAY

The streets of Amsterdam are congested with traffic. Cars, trucks, and buses battle for the right of way. But beside the lanes for motor vehicles run special lanes reserved for bicycles. Amsterdam has some 550,000 bicycles for its 700,000 people.

Many of the bikes ridden in Amsterdam are old and battered. Bicycle theft is rampant. A shiny new bike is all too likely to disappear. During the 1970s, the city launched a unique "public bicycle" program. Hundreds of white bicycles were placed on the streets. Anyone could pick one up, ride it, and leave it on the pavement for the next user. Unfortunately, the program was short-lived. Thieves collected the white bicycles, repainted them, and sold them illegally.

Doomed though it was, the white bicycle program shows Amsterdam's eagerness to meet the needs of all its citizens. Generous social programs ensure that the hungry are fed and the sick receive medical care. Very few people in Amsterdam are

So many Amsterdammers ride bicycles that the city has special bicycle lanes beside the traffic lanes for motor vehicles.

Houseboats on the Amstel River

homeless. Those who cannot afford to pay rent can live in housing funded by the government.

During the 1950s, however, Amsterdam had far fewer apartments than it needed. Waiting lists stretched for years. Many families lived on houseboats while they waited for an apartment to become available. Some found that they actually preferred this way of life. Today, about 2,500 houseboats are moored in the harbor or on the canals. Some are luxurious, complete with game rooms and roof gardens. Others are little more than floating sheds. Environmentalists worry that the houseboats add to pollution in the canals. In this city of waterways, however, nothing seems more natural than living on the water. Houseboats have come to stay.

Dutch philosopher Erasmus once wrote that Amsterdammers "are the only people on earth who live in the treetops." Erasmus referred to the fact that nearly all of Amsterdam rests on wooden posts. These posts, nearly 5 million of them, are made from tree trunks. Driven deep into the marshy soil, they form a solid foundation for Amsterdam's streets and buildings. So, as Erasmus put it long ago, the people of Amsterdam live on the tops of trees.

LAND FROM BENEATH THE WATERS

Sometime around the year A.D. 1275, a group of fishermen built a dam across the Amstel River in the present-day country called the Netherlands. As the years passed, the small fishing village beside the dam became a thriving town, and then a city. The city was known as Amstelledamme, or Amsterdam, named for the dam on the river. Today's Dam Square marks the spot where the original dam once stood.

From the city's earliest days, the people of Amsterdam found ways to alter their watery surroundings. They dammed rivers and dug canals. They built walls, or dikes, around lakes. Then they pumped out the water from behind the dikes to create more land. These reclaimed land areas are known as *polders*. They were once protected by walls made of poles.

Windmills like the ones shown in these pictures were used to drain water from the land to create polders.

These early Amsterdam farmers brought their goods to market in dogcarts, in baskets carried on yokes (shoulder bars), or in boats that were towed along the canals.

Amstel (AHM-STULL)
polder (POLE-DUHR)
Cornelis de Houtman (CORE-NAY-LISS DUH HOWT-MAHN)

The Dutch merchant ship Fortuna *on its way to the East in 1595*

Surrounded as they were by water, the people of Amsterdam naturally took to the sea. Fishing boats set out early each morning. In the evening, they returned, heavy with the catch of the day. Soon, Amsterdammers began to trade with other cities along the coast. As time passed, their voyages carried them farther and farther from home.

In 1595, a daring sea captain named Cornelis de Houtman sailed from Amsterdam on a voyage of exploration. For two long years, no word came back from de Houtman and his crew. Sadly, their families gave them up for lost.

Then, one day in 1597, extraordinary news swept through the streets of Amsterdam. Captain de Houtman was back! He had sailed all the way around southern Africa to the legendary South Seas. De Houtman's expedition had opened a trade route to the faraway islands of the East Indies. Amsterdam entered an exciting new era of trade, adventure, and prosperity.

THE GOLDEN AGE

During the 1600s, the Netherlands founded colonies in South Africa, South America, the West Indies, and present-day Indonesia. In North America, the Dutch established a tiny settlement on an island at the mouth of the Hudson River. They called this village New Amsterdam. New Amsterdam grew to become today's mighty New York City.

Amsterdam was the heart of a vast colonial empire. Immense riches flowed in from all over the world. Engineers constructed a great semicircle of canals to carry goods through the city. Wealthy merchants built elegant homes along the canals. Even the almshouses for the poor had lovely courtyards with gardens and statues.

During Amsterdam's Golden Age, painting flourished. Some of the world's finest artists captured the life of the city on canvas. Amsterdam's most noted painter was Rembrandt van Rijn (1606-1669), who came to the city in 1631. Rembrandt, as he is usually called, painted landscapes, historical scenes, and pictures with Biblical themes.

Rembrandt van Rijn
(REMM-BRAHNT VAHN RAIN)

Rembrandt self-portrait

This painting shows the Dutch fleet during a 1667 naval war with England.

He is best known for his remarkable portraits. Instead of mere physical beauty, Rembrandt's paintings convey a person's inner character. In his painting *The Night Watch,* he depicts a group of militia men. Each man in the painting comes fully to life.

Amsterdam's Golden Age lasted for less than a century. A series of wars finally weakened the city. Yet the canals, the grand buildings, and the paintings of the great Dutch masters remain. They are enduring memories of the days when Amsterdam seemed to rule the world.

An early view of Amsterdam

ENEMIES AND REBELS

In 1806, Amsterdam's magnificent City Hall was transformed into a royal palace. It was not a Dutch monarch who sat on the throne. The Royal Palace was occupied by a French ruler named Louis Napoleon. Louis was installed in Amsterdam by his brother, the Emperor Napoleon Bonaparte, who had conquered most of Europe. The French ruled for only a few years. But the emperor's home on Dam Square is called the Royal Palace to this day.

During World War II, German forces invaded the Netherlands. Life was especially difficult for those people in areas that had been bombed and shelled. This Dutch housewife is trying to put together a meal in her shell-shattered kitchen.

The Dutch city of Rotterdam was nearly destroyed by German bombs during World War II. These German soldiers are leaving their car to inspect the ruins of the city.

More than a century later, the Netherlands fell under foreign rule once again. In 1940, early in World War II, German forces invaded Amsterdam. German dictator Adolf Hitler annexed the Netherlands to his growing empire. The German invasion was disastrous for Amsterdam's Jewish population. As many as 100,000 Jewish citizens were shipped to concentration camps in Eastern Europe. About 70,000 lost their lives.

Many Amsterdammers resisted the German occupation, putting their own lives in peril. In February 1941, dockworkers and city employees organized a general strike. The strikers protested the treatment of the city's Jews at German hands. For days, all shipping ceased. Trams and buses stood still. At last, the strike collapsed when the Germans rounded up its leaders. To teach rebellious Amsterdam a lesson, the strikers were shot.

Many Jews and protesters tried to survive by "diving." With the help of sympathetic friends, "divers" went into hiding, sometimes for many years. Those who helped them hide and supplied them with food lived in constant danger.

In the summer of 1942, a Jewish businessman named Otto Frank went into hiding with his wife, his teenage daughters Margot and Anne, and four others. For more than two years, the Franks lived in a secret room behind Otto Frank's former office. Only a revolving bookcase concealed the entrance to their hidden retreat. During the years of fear and isolation, Anne Frank kept a diary. She recorded the daily happenings of her life, and her thoughts about the world she lived in. On July 15, 1944, she wrote, "In spite of everything, I still believe that people are really good at heart." Three weeks later, the Germans discovered the family's hiding place. The Franks were taken to a concentration camp, where Anne died a few weeks before the end of the war.

During the German occupation, all Jews in Amsterdam had to wear a yellow Star of David bearing the word "Jood" (Jew).

Frank family members are shown here in July 1941, before they were forced to go into hiding during the German occupation. From right to left: Margot Frank, her mother Edith, Anne, Otto Frank, Otto Frank's mother. (The older man and the young child in front have not been identified.)

Anne Frank

During the winter of 1944-1945, a terrible food and fuel shortage gripped Amsterdam and much of the Netherlands. People burned their chairs and tables in an effort to keep warm. The city's cats and dogs disappeared, sold by butchers as "roof rabbits." Before the winter was over, some 20,000 Netherlanders died.

After the war, Amsterdam's population swelled. Suddenly, housing was in short supply. The government encouraged people to rent out spare rooms to people without homes. Many homeless people became "squatters," taking over abandoned buildings.

In the 1960s and 1970s, thousands of young people poured into Amsterdam from all over Europe and the United States. They camped in the parks and sang in the streets. At the same time, immigrant workers from Morocco, Turkey, and Indonesia streamed into the city. Yet Amsterdam managed to overlook differences. Somehow the city made room for everyone.

A Sorrowful Reminder

Each year, hundreds of thousands of visitors are drawn to the famous house where Anne Frank hid during World War II. They climb the steep, winding stairs, and squeeze through a narrow doorway concealed behind a bookcase. There it is, the tiny, secret apartment that was Anne Frank's whole world for more than two years. The walls are still decorated with pictures that Anne herself pasted up. Her famous diary was found on the floor after the family was captured and taken away.

In 1865, an American writer named Mary Mapes Dodge published *Hans Brinker, or the Silver Skates*, a novel for children. *Hans Brinker* portrays a Dutch boy who skates everywhere he goes along frozen canals. Actually, the canals of Amsterdam do not freeze every winter. When there is ice thick enough for skating, it lasts only a few weeks. The freezing of the canals is a great occasion. Schools and offices close. Everyone puts on skates. Skaters glide and race. At stands on the ice, they pause to enjoy hot chocolate.

Amsterdammers love celebrations. They don't need ice as an excuse to leave their troubles behind and have fun.

PEOPLE AND PARKS

"Heaven is our roof. We do not work. We are as free as birds." These words were written in the seventeenth century by Dutch poet Joost van den Vondel. Vondelpark, one of the most beloved parks in Amsterdam, is named in his honor. During the 1960s and 1970s, young people flocked to Amsterdam from all over the world. They camped in the parks, singing and playing as though life were a vast open-air party. They seemed to take van den Vondel's words very much to heart.

By the 1990s, Amsterdam's parks were no longer a scene of hippie revelry. Yet they still have the atmosphere of a glorious outdoor festival. Young and old, rich and poor—everyone is invited.

Below: A canalside park in the south of Amsterdam
Opposite page: Vondelpark

The "hippies" who came to Amsterdam in the 1960s and 1970s wore jewelry such as this.

Joost van den Vondel (YOHST VAHN DUH VAWN-DULL)
Vondelpark (VAWN-DULL-PARK)

A puppeteer entertains a child in an Amsterdam park.

In warm weather, the parks are alive with puppeteers, jugglers, mimes, and acrobats. Musicians delight the crowds with free performances on bongos, guitars, and other instruments. The parks are gathering places where something is always about to happen.

In the densely populated city, Amsterdamse Bos (Amsterdam Wood) offers a refreshing glimpse of nature. Covering 2,000 acres, it includes an artificial lake and 125 miles of hiking trails. The forest was created during the 1930s. At that time, the Netherlands, like the rest of the world, was mired in a

A mime artist in Dam Square

Amsterdamse Bos (AHM-STAIR-DAHM- SUH BAWSS)

terrible economic depression. The Dutch government launched the Amsterdam Wood project to make jobs for thousands of people who were out of work. The forest is planted on a polder, land formed by damming and draining a lake.

Above: The Vondelpark bandstand
Left: This Vondelpark statue has a place of honor in a grassy area.

TESTING THE BODY,
EASING THE MIND

Soccer is a major preoccupation in Amsterdam. Ajax, the city's professional team, is a powerhouse. Normally placid Amsterdammers turn passionate about Ajax, which has won several all-European championships. During the 1970s, Ajax was banned from competing for a year because its fans were so rowdy.

In the past, children spent their free time playing tag and jumping rope on the sidewalks. Today, the streets are congested with traffic. The pavement is no longer a safe playground. Organized activities have largely replaced free outdoor play.

Ajax, the famous Amsterdam soccer team, on a canal-boat victory tour of the city

After school and on weekends, girls and boys play soccer, tennis, and field hockey. Many take part in swimming or gymnastics competitions.

Amsterdammers enjoy a rich diet of meat, cheese, and creamy desserts. They delight in ethnic foods, from Indonesian meat and rice dishes to Italian pastas. Many shops specialize in chocolate, which comes in every possible color and design. Despite their love of good food, few Amsterdammers are overweight. Perhaps this is because they are physically active. Even if they do not play soccer or tennis, they are anything but couch potatoes. Amsterdammers hike, row, jog, bicycle, in-line skate, and work out at health clubs. When they shop or run errands, they often walk or ride a bicycle rather than drive a car.

Children fishing in an Amsterdam canal

Jumping rope used to be a popular activity for the children of Amsterdam.

Amsterdammers enjoy many outdoor activities, including rowing on the city's canals.

Vincent van Gogh
(VINN-SENT VAHN HOHH)
Concertgebouw
(CONE-SAIRT-HUH-BOW)
Melkweg (MELK-WEHH)

This self-portrait of Vincent van Gogh shows his bandaged ear.

Amsterdam is known for its vibrant art scene. On at least one notable occasion, however, the city failed to welcome a major new talent. In the early 1880s, Amsterdam's art critics rejected the work of a young painter named Vincent van Gogh (1853-1890). To the critics, Van Gogh's paintings seemed to make no sense. They depicted bleak scenes of poverty and pain. Yet their colors were brilliant, and the paintings shimmered with light.

Discouraged by the Amsterdam critics, Van Gogh moved to Paris and went on painting. His life was haunted by mental illness. Shortly before his death, he slashed off his own ear. Despite his personal tragedy, Van Gogh is now regarded as one of the finest painters of his time.

Today, Amsterdam gives generous support to its painters and sculptors. Many public buildings are decorated with murals. Public funds support art exhibitions throughout the year.

The interior of
Amsterdam's
concert hall, the
Concertgebouw.

In 1879, the great German composer Johannes Brahms conducted his Third Symphony in Amsterdam. After the concert, he told the Amsterdammers, "You are good people, but bad musicians." Brahms' remark spurred the city to establish a new symphony orchestra, the Concertgebouw. Today, the Royal Concertgebouw Orchestra of Amsterdam is considered one of the best orchestras in the world. Amsterdam also hosts the Netherlands Philharmonic and several chamber orchestras. If classical music is not to your liking, there is also the Melkweg, or Milky Way. A converted dairy, the Melkweg is a hall for rock concerts with an international flavor.

In June, Amsterdammers turn out by the thousands for the Holland Festival. The festival is a month-long extravaganza of concerts, plays, opera, and dance. It draws top performers from all over the world. The Holland Festival is one of many festivals and holidays that enliven the city throughout the year.

German composer Johannes Brahms (right) conducted a symphony in Amsterdam.

SPECIAL DAYS

Amsterdammers welcome the new year by gathering in Dam Square. The air rings with music from dozens of local bands. In addition to champagne, Amsterdammers enjoy sugary doughnuts, a special New Year treat.

April 30 is Queen's Day, the birthday of a former queen of the Netherlands. The day is marked by parades and patriotic speeches. But for most Amsterdammers, sidewalk sales are the best part of this holiday. Children and adults set out tables and sell all the cast-offs of the preceding year—old books, toys, clothes, cassette recordings. Nobody

Amsterdammers celebrating Queen's Day in Dam Square

goes home empty-handed. One person's junk is another person's treasure.

Every four years, in the month of August, dozens of tall ships glide into Amsterdam Harbor. Representing navies from all over the world, the ships come for a festival called "Sail Amsterdam." People crowd the wharves to admire their graceful hulls and towering masts. For a week, Amsterdam is swept back to the Golden Age of Sail.

A young girl riding an Amsterdam carousel

Music in the Streets

Here and there in central Amsterdam, the streets overflow with lively circus music. The music is produced by brightly painted barrel organs that stand on the sidewalks. These organs were once cranked by hand while the organ-grinder's trained monkey collected coins from passersby. Most of today's organs run on gasoline, but the sparkling music is still the same.

On a Saturday in September, the people of Amsterdam line the streets to watch the Bloemen Corso, or Flower Parade. Huge floats buried in flowers cross the city. The parade ends at Dam Square. The Netherlands is the world's leading exporter of cut flowers, and the Flower Parade is a glorious celebration of the floral trade.

For hundreds of years, children in Amsterdam set out their shoes for St. Nicholas on the night of December 5. St. Nicholas filled the shoes of all good children with oranges, candy, and small toys. Bad children received a just reward for their wicked ways—they got lumps of coal or bundles of switches for spankings. Today, St. Nicholas still visits many homes in Amsterdam. But video games,

Bloemen Corso (BLOOM-uh CORE-zoh)

A colorful float in Amsterdam's Bloemen Corso (Flower Parade)

A 1905 painting of an Amsterdam canal with St. Nicholas Church in the background

CDs, and other modern presents are too big to fit in the average shoe. In recent decades, American-style Christmas has caught on throughout the city. Amsterdam children have not one, but two chances to give and receive longed-for presents in December. Like the children they see in American movies and television shows, they celebrate Christmas on December 25. And on December 5, they set out their shoes for St. Nicholas. St. Nicholas, like so much else from medieval Amsterdam, remains very much alive.

A Dutch cocoa tin

PRESENT

I f Rembrandt traveled through time and suddenly found himself in central Amsterdam today, he would feel very much at home. Car traffic has certainly changed the landscape. But Rembrandt would recognize most of the buildings and the layout of the streets and canals. If Rembrandt touched down on the outskirts of Amsterdam, however, he would be utterly lost. He would see glass-and-steel buildings taller than any he ever imagined. He would be baffled by a mystifying tangle of superhighways. Where he remembered lakes and bays, he would find dry land.

The face of Amsterdam has changed dramatically since the Golden Age. Yet Amsterdam has never ceased to be a city of art and excitement. It is a city of waterways, the cultural heart of the Netherlands.

THE FRINGE AND BEYOND

In Amsterdam's western harbor lie three artificial islands. The Western Islands, as they are called, were created with landfill during the 1630s. To prevent fires within the city, the islands were used for the storage of gunpowder. Today, many of the old storehouses have been turned into apartments and artist's lofts. Marshy areas on the islands are a perfect habitat for ducks and herons.

Amsterdam's largest nature area is the Amsterdamse Bos, or Amsterdam Wood, on the southwestern edge of the city. Exhibits in the Bos Museum explain how this park was made during the Great Depression of the 1930s. The museum also displays examples of the wood's diverse plants and animals.

Costumed Dutch children next to a Holland tulip display bed

During the 1600s, the Dutch people developed a passion for tulips. Merchants made and lost fortunes by investing in prized tulip bulbs. The Netherlands still leads the world in the flower industry. The largest flower market on earth is at Aalsmeer, just outside the city near Schiphol Airport. The size of 100 football fields, the Aalsmeer Flower Market is the world's largest commercial building. Potted plants and huge bundles of cut flowers are auctioned off to international traders. Visitors who watch the bidding from catwalks around the main gallery breathe the fragrance of a million blossoms.

A colored photogravure of an early Amsterdam flower market

Holland tulips

Aalsmeer (AHLSS-MARE)
Schiphol (SS-HIPP-HAWL)

For centuries, the fishing village of Marken stood on a tiny island north of Amsterdam. Then, in 1957, a causeway linked Marken with the mainland. Houses are built on stilts because Marken was often flooded. To the delight of tourists, the people of Marken still wear the traditional costumes of their ancestors. Foreign visitors love to have their pictures taken as they try on wooden shoes and starched caps.

Typical houses in the Dutch fishing village of Marken

The people of Marken still wear the traditional Dutch clothing of their ancestors, including starched caps, aprons, and wooden shoes. This woman is shown inside her home.

Marken (MAHRK-UH)

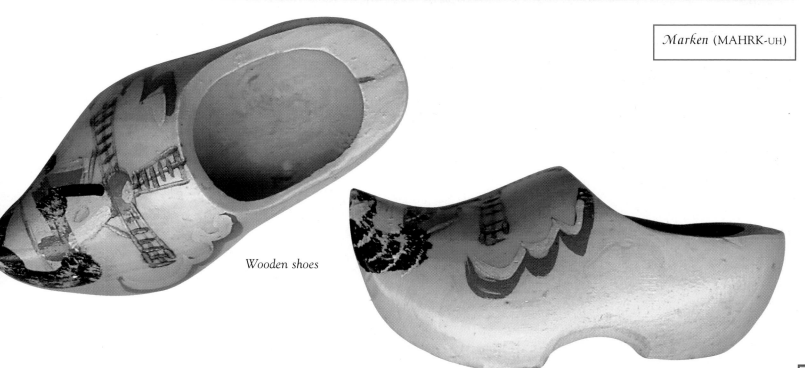

Wooden shoes

THE NEW CITY

In 1612, work began on Amsterdam's three main canals. The canals curved around the central part of the city. Today, the area within the canals is called the "Old City." The "New City" is the area outside the canals. How old is "old"? How new is "new"? Parts of the "new" city date all the way back to the seventeenth century.

Two canals, the Keisersgracht and Reguliersgracht, intersect at this corner.

Left: The 300-year-old Skinny Bridge is one of Amsterdam's most cherished landmarks. Below: Tourists view the canal houses of Amsterdam from the deck of a canal boat.

Amsterdam's three major canals loop around the old city in concentric semicircles. Like a series of cross streets, smaller canals link the main ones together. Hundreds of fine old houses stand along the canals, relics of Amsterdam's Golden Age. The best way to view the canal houses is from the

deck of a boat. Every half hour, canal boats filled with sightseers leave from designated spots around the city.

Some canal houses have been divided into apartments, and others are used as office buildings. By modern standards, canal houses are impractical. Their rooms are small and narrow, and they have steep, treacherous stairways. From the outside, however, these houses are strikingly handsome. In Amsterdam, they have monument status. This means that it is against the law to change their outward appearance.

The most elegant houses flank a stretch of canal called the Golden Bend. Near the Golden Bend district is the Museum Quarter. Amsterdam has a wealth of museums, and some of its finest ones are found here. Built to resemble a palace, the Rijksmuseum houses a splendid collection of paintings and sculptures. Its 250 rooms display works of art from the Middle Ages to modern times. Rembrandt's best-known painting, *The Night Watch,* holds a place of honor.

The Van Gogh Museum also stands in the Museum Quarter. It is a tribute to Vincent van Gogh, the painter who was once rejected by Amsterdam's art circle. Another landmark in the Museum Quarter is the Stedelijk Museum. It exhibits an outstanding collection of modern art.

Much of Amsterdam's old Jewish Quarter was destroyed during World War II. After the war, new

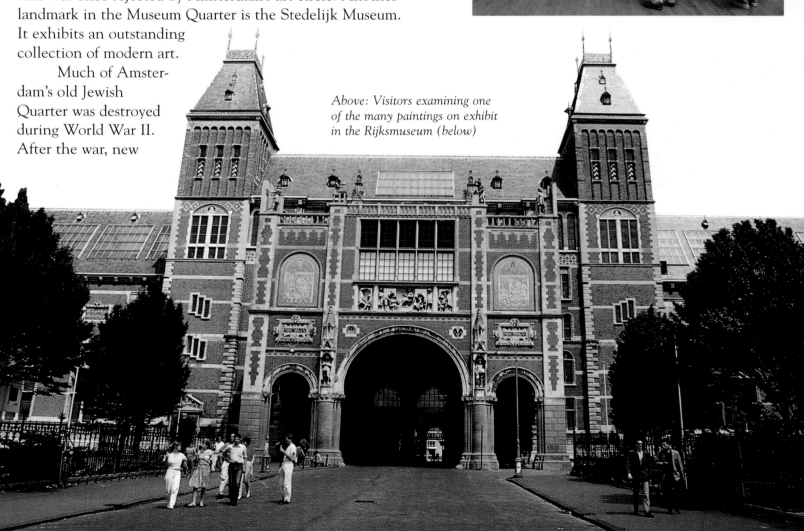

Above: Visitors examining one of the many paintings on exhibit in the Rijksmuseum (below)

apartments sprang up where old buildings had been leveled. A leading attraction of the Jewish Quarter is the Jewish Historical Museum. It is housed in a complex of four beautiful old synagogues that are connected by covered walkways. Displays in the museum recall Jewish life in Amsterdam, beginning in the 1500s. Photographs and other mementos tell the tragic story of Amsterdam's Jewish people during the war years.

During the seventeenth century, Amsterdam ruled on the high seas. The Maritime Museum is a reminder of the city's glorious days of sail. Early maps and globes show Dutch explorations in Africa, the Americas, and the South Seas. Several restored sailing vessels float in the harbor.

The restored United East Indian Company ship Amsterdam *is anchored in the harbor of the Maritime Museum.*

Gable Art

The peaked roofs of Amsterdam's canal houses are adorned with gables and balustrades. Many of the gables have carvings that hint at the work done by the house's owners. A blacksmith's house shows a man at a forge. A miller's house displays sheaves of wheat. These carved signs acted as addresses in the days before houses were numbered.

Rijksmuseum (RAKES-MOO-ZAY-UMM)
Stedelijk (STAY-DUH-LUCK)

THE OLD CITY

Every fifteen minutes, chimes float over the oldest section of Amsterdam. The chimes come from a stone tower called the Munttoren. The Munttoren is one of the last traces of the wall that surrounded Amsterdam in the Middle Ages.

Many of the buildings of central Amsterdam have stood for centuries. The famous Central Station, on the other hand, was completed in 1885. The building looks more like a palace than a train station. The station stands on a polder, land reclaimed from the city's medieval harbor.

Above: Amsterdam's Central Station, completed in 1885, looks more like a palace than a train station.

Left: A colorful tram in front of Central Station

Damrak, the main avenue in the old city, leads to Dam Square. East of Damrak lies a district called the Old Side, which was settled in the thirteenth century. The New Side, west of Damrak, was built 100 years later.

On the western side of Dam Square stands the New Church, built in 1490. Opposite the New Church is the National Monument, a memorial to those who died in World War II. The monument contains urns of earth from

The New Church was built in 1490.

*Sisters dressed for the rain share
a secret in Dam Square.*

Indonesia and each of the 12 provinces of the Netherlands.

Amsterdam's Royal Palace looms above Dam Square. The Royal Palace holds a special place in the hearts and minds of the people of Amsterdam. It stands as a symbol of the Golden Age, when it was the finest City Hall in all Europe. It speaks of the long-standing traditions that prevail in Amsterdam, this oldest and newest of cities.

Munttoren (MOOHN-TORE-UH)

FAMOUS LANDMARKS

The Anne Frank House

The Aalsmeer flower auction

The Royal Palace

Royal Palace
Ceremonial palace on Dam Square. This magnificent building was completed in 1655 to serve as Amsterdam's City Hall. In 1806, it briefly became the palace of Emperor Louis Napoleon. On display are paintings, sculptures, and furniture from the seventeenth century.

Rembrandt's House
Home of Rembrandt van Rijn, Amsterdam's most celebrated painter. Many of Rembrandt's etchings and drawings are on exhibit. Rembrandt, who went into debt to buy expensive furnishings for his home, died in poverty.

Rijksmuseum
Amsterdam's leading museum of art. The museum houses more than 1 million pieces. Collections include paintings by seventeenth-century European masters, works of Asian art, and seventeenth-century dollhouses. Rembrandt's painting *The Night Watch* holds a place of honor.

Van Gogh Museum
Tribute to painter Vincent van Gogh. About 200 paintings by Van Gogh are on display, as well as works by many other noted artists of his era. Much of the collection was a gift to the national government from Van Gogh's nephew.

Maritime Museum
Museum on the Eastern Harbor. Exhibits recall Amsterdam's days of glory on the high seas. Visitors can explore several fully restored sailing vessels. The main building was once a warehouse for the Dutch Admiralty, and was patrolled by hundreds of cats.

Anne Frank House
The house where Anne Frank and her family hid for two years during World War II. Visitors can climb the twisting stairs and squeeze through the secret door into the Frank family's hiding place. Anne's famous diary was found on the floor after the family was discovered by the Germans.

The Maritime Museum

The Van Gogh Museum

Albert Cuypstraat
Picturesque outdoor market along a street in the Pijp District. Stalls display foods, clothing, and handi-crafts that reveal Amsterdam's rich ethnic diversity.

Aalsmeer Flower Market
The largest commercial flower market in the world. Visitors can watch from catwalks as dealers bid on huge bundles of cut blossoms. Prices start high and work their way down until a dealer makes a bid.

Marken
Fishing village outside Amsterdam. Once on an island, Marken is now linked to the mainland by a causeway. Marken thrives on tourism. People still wear the traditional costumes that have disappeared in most other parts of the Netherlands.

Central Station
Central railway station for Amsterdam. The station was built in 1889 by Dutch architect P. J. H. Cuypers. It resembles a medieval castle. Central Station is one of Amsterdam's major landmarks.

Old Church
Also called Saint Nicholas Church, it is the oldest church in Amsterdam. The earliest surviving portion was built in 1334, about 100 years before the "New Church" was constructed on Dam Square. The Old Church is nearly hidden by the chapels and houses that have been added over the years.

Tripp House
One of Amsterdam's most famous canal houses. It was built in the 1660s by the Tripp brothers, who made their fortune in the weapons industry. The chimneys are shaped like small cannons.

Skinny Bridge
One of Amsterdam's most cherished landmarks. This 300-year-old bridge over the Amstel River is named after an earlier bridge, which was exceptionally narrow.

FAST FACTS

POPULATION   1993

City   713,400

Metropolitan Area   950,000

LOCATION Amsterdam is the cultural capital of the Netherlands; The Hague is the political capital, or seat of government. Amsterdam is built on some 90 islands, connected by 600 bridges. The North Sea lies to the west. To the east is the IJ, a branch of the lake called the IJsselmeer. The Amstel River once flowed through Amsterdam, but today much of its length has been dammed and diverted.

CLIMATE Amsterdam lies in the temperate zone, and the climate has few extremes. In July, temperatures average 77 degrees Fahrenheit. The average January temperatures is 30 degrees Fahrenheit.

GOVERNMENT The city government of Amsterdam is headed by a mayor, or *Burgomaster*, appointed by the crown. The City Council, or lawmaking body, has 45 members, who are elected to four-year terms.

ECONOMY Financial services lead Amsterdam's economy. These include the banking, insurance, and investment industries. Among Amsterdam's manufactured products are aircraft, electronic equipment, processed foods, chemicals, and steel. Amsterdam is the world's largest distributor of cut flowers. The city is also a leading center in the diamond-processing industry. Diamonds are cut and shaped for jewelry and for industrial use. Shipping is also a leading industry. However, the nearby city of Rotterdam is the biggest and busiest port in the Netherlands.

CHRONOLOGY

About 1275
Fishermen dam the Amstel River and found the village of Amstelledamme, later called Amsterdam.

1452
Fire destroys much of the town; new laws require brick and tile in building instead of timber.

1515
The Netherlands becomes part of the Roman Catholic Spanish Empire.

1579
A treaty called the Union of Utrecht separates the region that today is the Netherlands from Belgium.

1585
Antwerp, in present-day Belgium, falls to Roman Catholic Spain; many wealthy Protestant merchants flee to Amsterdam.

1597
Cornelis de Houtman opens a trade route between Amsterdam and the East Indies (present-day Indonesia).

1602
The Dutch East India Company is established to coordinate trade between the Netherlands and the Far East.

1612
Work begins on three major canals in central Amsterdam.

1642
Rembrandt completes his famous painting *The Night Watch*.

1660
Amsterdam's population reaches 220,000.

1655
Amsterdam's City Hall (later turned into the Royal Palace) is completed.

Dutch boy and tulips

1795
In the "Velvet Revolution," French troops invade Amsterdam in a bloodless takeover.

1806
Emperor Louis Napoleon takes the throne of the Netherlands; he turns Amsterdam's City Hall into the Royal Palace.

1848
The Netherlands undergoes democratic reform after riots in Amsterdam; a new kind of Parliament is established.

1889
Amsterdam's magnificent Central Station is completed.

1928
Amsterdam hosts the Olympic Games.

1940
Germany invades Amsterdam and takes over the Netherlands.

1941
Dock workers and municipal workers in Amsterdam strike to protest German treatment of Jewish citizens.

1942
Anne Frank and her family go into hiding.

1944-1945
Some 20,000 people die in the Netherlands due to shortages of food and fuel.

1945
Amsterdam is liberated from German occupation.

1963
Squatters protest against housing shortage in Amsterdam.

1990
Amsterdam receives a record number of visitors for an exhibition of Van Gogh's paintings; the exhibition marks the 100th anniversary of the artist's death.

AMSTERDAM

A B C C D E F G

1

2

JORDAAN

3

Amsterdam Harbor

Central Station

Anne Frank House

Old Church
(St. Nicholas Church)

4

New Church

Damrak

Maritime Museum

Royal Palace

Dam Square

National Monument

5

Tripp House

EASTERN HARBOR

OLD CITY

NEW CITY

Golden Bend

Rembrandt's House

6

City Hall

JEWISH QUARTER

Prinsengracht

Keizersgracht

Herengracht

Singel

Munttoren

Jewish Historical Museum

Melkweg

7

Skinny Bridge

Rijksmuseum

Amstel River

Tropical Museum

8

Stedelijk Museum

Van Gogh Museum

MUSEUM QUARTER

9

Concertgebouw

Albert Cuypstraat

10

PIJP

Singelgracht

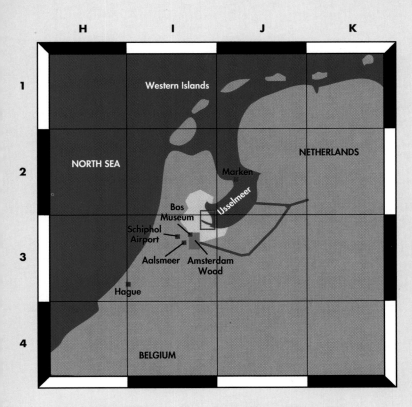

AMSTERDAM AND SURROUNDINGS

GLOSSARY

almshouse: Home for the poor and sick

annex: To add on

atone: To make up for, make amends

balustrade: Ornamental railing

causeway: Raised pathway across water or marshes

cupola: Small dome on a roof

gable: Decorative extension of a peaked roof

intimate: Close, personal

Middle Ages: Historical period in Europe between the A.D. 400s and 1500s

ornate: Elaborate, highly decorated

polder: A Dutch word meaning "land reclaimed from a lake or the sea"

prestigious: Giving high status

rampant: Out of control, as in an epidemic

revelry: Jovial good times

switch: A slender stick used for spanking

tolerant: Accepting of differences

turret: Small tower

Picture Identifications

Cover: Houseboats on an Amsterdam Canal, children on a tricycle wagon, tulips
Title Page: Face painting at an Amsterdam street festival
Pages 4-5: The Royal Palace
Pages 8-9: Beautiful gabled townhouses along the Herengracht
Pages 20-21: Painting by Jan Brueghel of an early Dutch fish market (*Fishmarkt am Meeresstrand*)
Pages 30-31: Children skating on a frozen Amsterdam canal
Pages 44-45: Central Station

Photo Credits ©:

INDEX

Page numbers in boldface type indicate illustrations

TO FIND OUT MORE

BOOKS

Bailey, Donna. *Netherlands*. Where We Live series. Austin, Texas: Steck-Vaughn Company, 1992.

Christmas in the Netherlands. Chicago: World Book-Childcraft International, Inc., 1981.

Frank, Anne. *The Diary of a Young Girl*. New York: Doubleday, 1995.

Harris, Nathaniel. *The Art of Van Gogh*. New York: Gallery Books, 1982.

Ippisch, Hanneke. *Sky: A True Story of Resistance During World War II*. New York: Simon & Schuster Books for Young Readers, 1996.

Kristensen, Preben and Fiona Cameron. *We Live in the Netherlands*. New York: The Bookwright Press, 1985.

Netherlands in Pictures. Visual Geography series. Minneapolis: Lerner Publications Co., 1991.

Schwartz, Gary. *Rembrandt*. First Impressions series. New York: Harry N. Abrams, Inc., 1992.

Sherrow, Victoria. *Amsterdam*. Cities at War series. New York: New Discovery Books, 1992.

Verhoeven, Rian. *Anne Frank, Beyond the Diary: A Photographic Remembrance*. New York: Viking, 1993.

ONLINE SITES

Amsterdam
http://pmwww.cs.vu.nl/public_service/Amsterdam/
General information, clickable color photos, maps, neighborhood tours, museums, theaters, dance, music, and plenty more

Amsterdam
http://qqq.com/holland/amsterdam.html
Learn about Amsterdam's government, visit museums, cafes, and parks, and see a real-time picture of the IJ River

Amsterdam: The Berkeley Guides
http://www.loci.com/HO/travel/Berkeley/AmsterMain.html
Lots of information on the city, along with things to see and do and tips on traveling

The Amsterdam Channel
http://channels.nl/adam.html
Take a tram or walking tour of Amsterdam! Visit many different sites and learn about the city's people. Complete with photos and maps

Amsterdam: The Essentials
http://www.nbt.nl/NBT-amst-index.html
The Van Gogh Museum, clickable images of canal scenes, entertainment, restaurants, concerts, ballet, and more

City.net: Amsterdam
http://www.city.net/countries/netherlands/amsterdam/travel_and_attractions
City information, yellow and white pages, arts and entertainment, weather, sightseeing, and maps

Holland: City Index
http://www.xxLINK.nl/cities/
Get information and links for hundreds of cities in the Netherlands, including Amsterdam

The Internet Guide to Amsterdam
http://www.cwi.nl/~steven/amsterdam.html
Amsterdam—its language, money, transportation, shopping, news, places to see, maps, and links to other sites

Van Gogh Museum
http://www.gallery-guide.com/museum/vangogh/
Learn about Van Gogh's life and see many of his paintings, presented as clickable/expandable photos

ABOUT THE AUTHOR

Deborah Kent grew up in Little Falls, New Jersey, and received a B.A. in English from Oberlin College. She earned a master's degree from Smith College School for Social Work. After working for four years at the University Settlement House in New York City, she moved to San Miguel de Allende in central Mexico. There she wrote her first young-adult novel, *Belonging*.

Ms. Kent is the author of more than a dozen young-adult novels, as well as numerous nonfiction titles for children. She lives in Chicago with her husband, children's book author R. Conrad Stein, and their daughter Janna. She has visited Amsterdam twice and finds it a fascinating city, particularly because her mother's family came from the Netherlands.